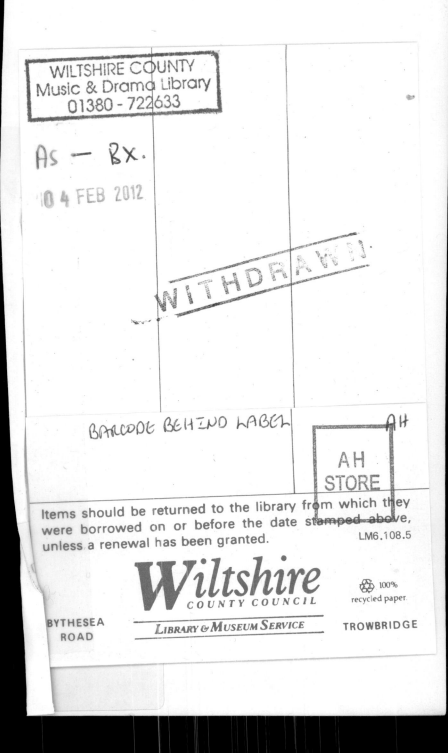

THE DREAM OF CHIEF CRAZY HORSE

The Dream of
Chief Crazy Horse

DAVID POWNALL

FABER AND FABER
3 Queen Square
London

First published in 1975
by Faber and Faber Limited
3 Queen Square London WC1
Printed in Great Britain by
Whitstable Litho, Straker Brothers Ltd

ISBN 0 571 10672 2 (hard bound edition)
ISBN 0 571 10673 0 (paper covers)

CONDITIONS OF SALE

For ANDREW DALE SANDERS

No matter how difficult the road,
I will be there: outlasting all wars,
all fire, all hunts, wounds and separations:
enduring as the old earth endures,
strongly, without fear:
I will be here
with you, befriending.
Unending.

from the Oglala Sioux

This play was commissioned by Rossall Junior School, Fleetwood. The first performance was staged at the Museum Theatre on November 28th 1973 and directed by Tony Brunskill.

CHARACTERS

GENERAL CROOK	FRIAR DE VALVERDE
CRAZY HORSE	JACQUES CARTIER
THE PEOPLE	SIR WALTER RALEIGH
COLUMBUS	PETER MINUIT
SAILORS	TWO INDIANS
THE TAINOS	EMIGRANTS
ARAWAK INDIAN	4 WAMPANOAGS
CORTES	SLAVES
TWO CONQUISTADORS	METACOMET
AMBASSADOR	FRENCH ESTATE AGENT
INTERPRETER	MEXICAN GENERAL
MONTEZUMA	LITTLE CROW
CACIQUE	BLACK KETTLE
CITIZENS OF	MANGAS COLORADO
CEMPOALLA	WOVOKA
5 AZTEC TRIBUTE-	CAPTAIN JACK
COLLECTORS	SATANTA
HEADMEN OF CHOLULA	QUANAH PARKER
PRIEST	JOSEPH
BEARERS	SPOTTED TAIL
THE INCA	BIG FOOT
PIZARRO	STANDING BEAR

CHIEF-IN-HEAD	THE BUFFALO
HUMPED OVER	SITTING BULL
JUDGE DUNDY	AUCTIONEER

ACT ONE

SET: the stage has two acting levels, upper and
lower. Dominating the upper level is a large physical map of the Americas from Cape Horn to Alaska,
including the Chukchi Peninsula of Western Siberia.
The map must have no political frontiers, towns or
man-made designations - only the mountain ranges,
rivers, lakes, valleys and plains. As the audience
enter the theatre this map is illuminated by the
reflected light of a full moon which is suspended
above it.

The lower acting level should be at floor level
with the first row of the auditorium. To right and
left the lower level develops into two alcoves. The
stage R alcove is backed by Stars and Stripes. There
is a camp stool and a folding table as used by comm-
anders in the field. A piano stands at the back of the
alcove.

The stage L alcove is backed by a par-fleche
shield and a war-lance hung with feathers. An assort-
ment of drums and rattles is stacked against the
wall. A colourful blanket is spread on the floor.

Only the moon shines. Slowly it dims to total

BLACKOUT. At the moment when the audience begins to fall silent, a figure pads along the aisle from the rear of the auditorium. He should feel his way forward, step by step. It is CRAZY HORSE, war chief of the Oglala Sioux.

CRAZY HORSE: Shush! Shush! Shush! You are in my dream now. Sleep with me, quiet, shush! Share my dream. Be with me. Help me. Dream. (Silence. Then a loud neighing of a horse. CRAZY HORSE jumps. The horse sounds wild, fearful. The moon-light comes up just enough to show CRAZY HORSE cavorting up the aisle as if he is riding a wild horse.) Hey! Hey! What a horse! See him buck and prance! This is the horse in my dream. I ride him night after night across plain and hill ! Hey! Hey! This is my dream-horse. I have not got his government. (CRAZY HORSE mimes dismounting from the wild horse.) And so my friends gave me this name, Crazy Horse. I cannot ride him because he is me. You are part of Crazy Horse's dream for one night and we will see who is the horse. In my dream I can choose my enemy and I can choose my friend. Tonight I choose to dream with you, and I choose to have up here with me my old opponent, General George Crook.

12

An army bugle sounds. Crashing of feet off-stage R. Enter GENERAL CROOK in full military uniform of United States Army 1886, wearing sabre and revolver. He marches directly to alcove R, halts, about-turns, salutes the stars and stripes, about turns, faces the audience.

Soft thudding of a single drum off-stage. CRAZY HORSE pads across to alcove L and sits cross-legged on the blanket. Drum stops.

CRAZY HORSE: I have been born, lived, and died.
Once I saw the world and now I do not see it. I dream and drag you into my dream. Which is the real world? The Crazy Horse? The Tame Horse? Which story runs straightest?
(CRAZY HORSE smiles, then jumps to his feet.)
I see you, General Crook Three-Star God Almighty!

GENERAL CROOK: I see you, Chief Crazy Horse.

CRAZY HORSE: You remember me?

GENERAL CROOK: I remember you.

CRAZY HORSE: I have brought you out to play all the Great White Fathers. How does that suit you?

GENERAL CROOK: It suits me well enough.

CRAZY HORSE: Hopo-hook-ahay! Let's go! Tell us how to say the passing of a white man's year.

GENERAL CROOK: January
February
March

13

April

May

June

July

August

September

October

November

December

CRAZY HORSE: We called it:-

The Moon Of The Strong Cold

The Moon When The Snow Drifts

The Moon Of The Red Grass Appearing

The Moon When The Ponies Shed

The Moon When The Green Grass Is Up

The Moon When The Cherries Are Ripe

The Moon When The Geese Lose Their Feathers

The Moon When The Deer Paw The Earth

The Moon Of The Drying Grass

The Moon Of The Wild Rice

The Moon Of The Rutting Deer

The Moon Of The Popping Trees

GENERAL CROOK: You never use one word when a
dozen will do.

CRAZY HORSE: The moon will look well with the
stars on your flag and on your shoulder. One
day you will have the sun as well. It would be
right for the white man to have the sun. It is the
colour of his god.

14

GENERAL CROOK: Dammit man, come on! Let's
get things going! You got me here! If you want
me in your dream then let's not waste my time.

CRAZY HORSE: Your people have thrived, Gray
Wolf, they cover the earth and they own it. Mine
are scattered, living in the shadows. I see no
Sioux where there is power. I only see my people
in the pictures that move and they are not as I
knew them. Where are my people?

GENERAL CROOK: Take no goddamned notice of
writers and scribblers. Stick to the Truth,
dammit! Stick to the Truth and you'll be okay.

CRAZY HORSE: It is my dream, Gray Wolf Three
Stars Almighty Crook. I asked you into my
dream to tell your story. But it is the dream of
Crazy Horse and it lives in his head.

GENERAL CROOK: That doesn't worry me. I can
look people in the eye.

CRAZY HORSE: There was a word always on your
lips, Gray Wolf - honesty.

GENERAL CROOK: Too damn right there was.
Honesty is the most important thing there is. If
a man is honest then he's all right.

CRAZY HORSE: Honesty we will have, even though
it cannot help the dead nations. Honesty is for
the white men. They have need of it now. Ghosts
do not need honesty. We will be honest for
honesty's sake.

(Off-stage a soft repetitive chant, "Hena Waci!

Hena Waci!" and the shuffling of many feet.
Lights dim. Huddled figures enter from rear of
auditorium, heads held low as if battling against
a freezing wind. Spot on the map. CRAZY HORSE
takes his lance and mounts the upper level. The
figures are the people. They shuffle round the
stage area, always moving. CRAZY HORSE
points to the Bering Strait, the sea between the
Chukchi and Seward peninsulas.)

Here's where The People crossed. We came
out of the cold land to the West, following the
beasts. We were hunters and wanderers and we
found a bridge of rock that stood in the seas in
those days. Why we came I do not know. Perhaps
our land had been taken from us in the West,
perhaps there were other peoples who made war
upon us, perhaps we got lost. But we came
across that bridge and we were the first!
Thousands upon thousands of turnings of the sun
and earth ago, millions of sleeps and wakings,
that was when we came into our New World. The
Great Spirit was with us, the Sun was our father
and the Earth was our mother. We were lucky
to find that bridge.

(CRAZY HORSE traces the routes with his lance.
The chanting quietens.)

There was ice on the world in those days and we
journeyed through the valleys south, always
south. Some stayed in the snow, others went

16

across to the east, some stayed on the plains, some in the forests, some in the wet places, some in the dry. We travelled to the very tip of this great land and we went into it to live. We saw that it belonged to no one but the Great Spirit and the Uncreated Creator who made the Great Spirit. It was only ours because we lived upon it. If we had only known the way of it, we would have got a paper from the Great Spirit . . . .

GENERAL CROOK (butting in): However, five hundred years ago, a new philosophy was abroad in Europe, far to the East. It was the beginning of the Age of Discovery, the Age of Humanism, the re-birth of civilisation. Men of restless mind and daring courage looked to the unfound lands . . .

CRAZY HORSE: Hena waci, hena waci. They come. They come. The People came but that was not coming enough. (THE PEOPLE shuffle off by several exits.) Five hundred years ago the Great Spirit's head hit the blanket, he forgot us and slumbered. The god of The People went to bed.

GENERAL CROOK: The Europeans believed that there was nothing to the west, across the Atlantic Ocean, except, in time, the east.

CRAZY HORSE: Only the whites would come looking for nothing, hoping it would change into something.

(Sea sounds, the creaking of timbers, crack of

17

sails, gulls. Bright daylight. COLUMBUS strides
to centre-stage, keeping with the roll of the ship,
a spy-glass in his hand. He scans the horizon.)

GENERAL CROOK: Our bridge was a ship's boards
and we came to find out, to see what lay at the
end of the world. Curiosity was the wind that
blew Columbus towards the islands . . . .

CRAZY HORSE: And gold for kings and queens.

GENERAL CROOK: Dammit, man, he came from a
society based on money which was based on
gold. He had been brought up to see things as
being useful or useless. He was a practical man.

CRAZY HORSE: He was a thief!

(THE SAILORS enter stage L and R and mime
crowding sail before a good wind. The sounds
of the ship's progress increase.)

SAILORS: Spain is far behind.

We can only find it

going forward, going forward.

We hope the world is round

and will bring us home again

to Spain.

COLUMBUS (looking through his spy-glass): Thank
God!

SAILORS: What do you see?

COLUMBUS: India! We have found the other route!
Thank God!

(COLUMBUS rides the ship's motion like a
sailor, his face ecstatic. THE SAILORS lower

18

a boat over the side (to the lower level), clamber
down rope ladders into it, take up the oars.
COLUMBUS boards the boat and stands in the
bow. THE SAILORS row strongly and sing.)

SAILORS: Praise to the Virgin

Star of the sea,

Praise to the Virgin

Motherly, motherly.

(Stage R appear THE TAINOS, looking towards
COLUMBUS and the mimed boat. As THE
SAILORS sing on, THE TAINOS run off-stage
and return with fruits and vegetables (potatoes,
pineapples, strawberries, beans, pumpkin),
pots of chocolate, tobacco leaves (some of THE
TAINOS are smoking pipes), and put them on
the shore. As COLUMBUS lands THE TAINOS
clap and shout.)

TAINOS: Here he comes

over from the East,

the white face

of the sun rising

(THE TAINOS shake COLUMBUS'S hands, and
the hands of THE SAILORS. They greet them
with great friendliness, pressing their gifts
upon them. As THE SAILORS and COLUMBUS
try out the new fruits and vegetables, THE
TAINOS crowded round them, CRAZY HORSE
speaks to the audience.)

CRAZY HORSE: Like most white men of his time,

19

after centuries of wars, rebellions, persecutions, plagues, famines and other unhappinesses, Christopher Columbus did not know where he was going, where he had arrived at, or where he had been when he had gone. But he knew one thing. He was going to be rich, as rich as the Indies. So we were called Los Indios, the Indians - as if there weren't enough Indians in the world already.

GENERAL CROOK (pointing to the map): But here is where he had landed, in the Caribbean, the island later named San Salvador. Columbus was impressed with his reception and wrote back to his King:-

(COLUMBUS moves aside from the crowd and mimes letter-writing (parchment, quill and sand).)

COLUMBUS: "When we landed on this island, the people gave us gifts. I have never encountered a better nation. They are peaceable and good-natured, love their neighbours as themselves, their conversation is sweet and gentle and always illustrated with a smile. Though it is true that they sometimes go about naked, their manners are at all times decorous and res-pectable."

(COLUMBUS puts the letter inside his shirt, then returns to THE SAILORS and THE TAINOS.)

It is time for us to sleep. (He mimes putting his

head on a pillow.)

(THE TAINOS bring out mats and beckon COL-
UMBUS to lie down. THE SAILORS and THE
TAINOS follow suit. Lights down, moon up.
When they are all asleep, COLUMBUS wakens
THE SAILORS.)

(whispering) Now we must return to Spain. I
want to take ten Indians to show the king, with
all their gods, gold and jewellery. Raid their
village while these are sleeping, then we will
take our hosts to the ship.

(THE SAILORS slip away. COLUMBUS sits
apart and waits. Distant cries, gunshots. THE
TAINOS stir but do not waken.)

CRAZY HORSE: The beginning.

GENERAL CROOK: Dammit, man, he had to prove
what he had found! Who would believe him without evidence?

CRAZY HORSE: Was he on trial?

COLUMBUS: They must be made to work, sow, be
industrious. I will return and see to it that they
adopt our ways.

(THE SAILORS return, loaded with plunder.
Then they wake THE TAINOS, tie them up, and
put them on board the boat. THE TAINOS are
bewildered but do not fight back. Their aston-
ishment is a paralysis.)

SAILORS: Heathens! Anti-Christs! Into the boat!
We will take you to the place where steel is made!

21

(THE SAILORS row the boat to the ship. As
they mime the oar-strokes, COLUMBUS speaks
to the audience.)

COLUMBUS: And so I returned to Spain, having
persuaded ten of my hosts to accompany me.
One of them died upon arrival, but not before
he was baptised a Christian. I am proud to be
able to say that I made it possible for the first
Red Indian to enter Heaven.
(THE SAILORS and THE TAINOS go out.
GENERAL CROOK gets to his feet. Lights up.
Day.)

GENERAL CROOK: The Spaniards returned and
consolidated their position in the Caribbean.
They were courageous, determined men.

CRAZY HORSE: They came back with guns. They
came back with priests. They came back with
smallpox. They came back to San Salvador and
robbed, burned, murdered, pillaged and sold
the people into slavery until the Tainos were
exterminated - to a man! Then they moved on to
the other islands where The People lived and
the story was the same again.
(Enter COLUMBUS with an ARAWAK INDIAN,
a native of the Bahamas. He stands centre
stage.)

COLUMBUS (to audience): Ladies and gentlemen,
today we have a splendid specimen of a Bahamas
Indian up for public auction. If you examine

22

your catalogue you will see that he is in his
prime, free from disease, suffers from no
physical disability except his heathen nature,
and has already proved his fertility by fathering
several children. I personally guarantee that he
will work under the whip and, who knows, his
buyer may be able to save him for Christ! Think
of that! A converted Indian is worth gold in
Heaven! Now what am I bid?

(From the back of the auditorium come the bids
that keep the auction moving. They must be
shouted clearly. COLUMBUS conducts the
auction with the rapid running speech of the
professional auctioneer.)

May we have a starter? Now who'll give me a
figure? One peso? One peso at the back! Now
any advance on one peso for this handsome
fellow! Let me hear it! You, sir? You look as
though you need some help around the house!
We can't let him go for one. Take him down!
Two pesos? I have two pesos from the side here!
Two pesos? This is ridiculous! Look at him!
Look at him! At the peak of fitness! Clean in
his habits! Decent! Do I hear three? Three?
Yes! At the back there! Three I hear! A wise
bid, sir! Three pesos for this paragon of a
slave! Are you all finished? You'll let him go
for one measly peso, sir? Going for the first
time . . . no? Yes! Four pesos I'm bid. What?

23

Three and a half? No half bids here, sir! We
have no half measures! Four pesos? Right!
Going for the first time at four! Going for the
second time at four! And . . . GONE!
(The ARAWAK INDIAN is conducted down the
aisle by COLUMBUS and handed over to the
buyer, who hands over the money. COLUMBUS
wanders back, throwing the coins in the air.)

CRAZY HORSE: So terrible was the life of The
People who lived on these islands once the
Spaniards had come, that they were driven to
mass suicide to escape from the Hell that the
slavers, soldiers and adventurers brought with
them. They got one side of the Christian story.
The Devil stalked through the Caribbean in
Toledo steel armour. Men and women abstained
from all sexual life in order that children
should not be born into this horror . . . .

GENERAL CROOK: The Spanish military presence
was enlarged and a series of fortified ports
was constructed. A regular mercantile traffic
began with the mother country. Then Mexico
was discovered . . . .

CRAZY HORSE: By a slaving-party. Now it was too
late. If we had known the future by learning
from this Spanish lesson, we would have built
a great wall across the Eastern Sea between
America and the islands.

GENERAL CROOK: Cortes, a commander of genius,

24

a diplomat of outstanding ability, landed at what
later was to be called Vera Cruz in 1519.

CRAZY HORSE: Montezuma, the Aztec emperor, a
man raised up above The People until he lived in
a world of his own, heard of the landing.
(CORTES and TWO CONQUISTADORS march up
the aisle from the rear of the auditorium, their
steel feet crashing to a military drum. MONTE-
ZUMA, in a golden robe, enters stage R,
covering up his ears. CORTES drills the TWO
CONQUISTADORS.)

CORTES: Halt! Draw swords! At the ready! Lunge!
Detach! Lunge! Detach! Lunge! Detach! At the
heart! Rest easy!
(The TWO CONQUISTADORS stand at ease, hands
folded on the pommels of their swords.)

CORTES: We will wait to see what the emperor of
this heathen country will say to my ambassador.
He is made of gold.
(Enter AMBASSADOR and INTERPRETER.)

MONTEZUMA (clapping): Goodbye.

INTERPRETER: The emperor, Lord of all, says
"goodbye".

AMBASSADOR: But I've only just arrived!

INTERPRETER: The emperor does everything back-
wards, sir. He is so far above ordinary men
that he cannot be expected to behave in the same
manner. He sees everything before it happens,
such are his godly powers. He knows you will go

25

eventually so he says "goodbye", to show that
your stay must end.

AMBASSADOR(with spirit): Well, I say "hello"!

INTERPRETER: The white-face says "hello".

MONTEZUMA: Stand up!

INTERPRETER: The emperor, Lord of all, says
"stand up"!

AMBASSADOR: I am standing up!

INTERPRETER: But you would have to stand up if
you were sitting down, which is what you must
do.

(The AMBASSADOR shakes his head and sits on
the floor.)

AMBASSADOR: Tell the emperor that my master,
Cortes, a son of Spain and subject of a king
across the Eastern Sea, wishes to see all the
wonders of Mexico and to visit the capital and
be received by Montezuma, the emperor, himself.

INTERPRETER: Emperor, Lord of all, this man
here has not got a master who is not called
Cortes who is not a subject of a king who is not
across the Eastern Sea, who does not want to
see the wonders that are not in Mexico and
would hate to visit the capital and be received
by Montezuma, the emperor, yourself.

(MONTEZUMA nods vigorously.)

The emperor, Lord of all, says no.

AMBASSADOR (holding his head in his hands): To

what? What is he saying?

MONTEZUMA: You would be most welcome.

INTERPRETER: You must go away.

MONTEZUMA: I will not give you gifts of treasure.

INTERPRETER: You must take Cortes all the gold
and silver you can carry.

MONTEZUMA: And you may stay here for ever.

INTERPRETER (sharply): And go back from whence
you came!

(MONTEZUMA claps. A treasure chest is
brought in and opened at the AMBASSADOR'S
feet. It is full of gold ornaments, silver, jewels.
The AMBASSADOR, still shaking his head,
takes the chest and leaves. MONTEZUMA looks
after him.)

MONTEZUMA: Hello.

(CORTES and the TWO CONQUISTADORS mount
the upper level. MONTEZUMA exits, nodding.)

GENERAL CROOK: And so Montezuma, the emperor
of the great Aztec civilisation, made an error
that was to bring down his empire and destroy
himself. He gave Cortes a glimpse of the wealth
of America.

CRAZY HORSE: He gave him a remedy for a disease
of the heart common in men from the East. He
gave him gold.

GENERAL CROOK: Cortes ignored Montezuma's
order, but he kept the treasure and put it in a
ship.

CRAZY HORSE: If I could do a trade with the Great Spirit: that I would never have been born if he had never cast gold into the ground, I would do it. I would mine all the gold in the Americas with my teeth and spit it into the sea.

GENERAL CROOK: Then they would dive for it.

CRAZY HORSE: You would dive for it. You cannot disown them, Gray Wolf, they are yours.

GENERAL CROOK (coming down off the upper level): I am a soldier, Crazy Horse, like yourself.

CRAZY HORSE: You are a man. Your soldier is only one of your arms and one of your legs. The rest is white man. There's gold in your pocket.

GENERAL CROOK (sitting on his camp stool: I obey orders.

(CORTES turns to the audience.)

CORTES: I was faced by an empire that appeared to be as large as that of my master King Philip. But was I afraid? Of course not. I had guns. I had man-eating dogs. I had armour. I had horses. I had experience. In addition, the Aztec empire was divided, as we found when we entered the city of Cempoalla.

(Enter CACIQUE OF CEMPOALLA.)

CACIQUE (in a state of terror): Two legs! Two legs! He has two legs! Two legs! Only two legs!

(Enter CITIZENS, who gather round CACIQUE pointing, shouting.)

CITIZENS: Two legs! Only two legs! Ah, only two!
28

CORTES (slapping each thigh): One! Two! That's
    all! Why is that such a marvel!
CACIQUE: We were told that you were four-legged
    giants with human halves. We saw you from a
    distance on the road and that is what you were.
    Now you are a man.
CORTES (aside to the audience): You see how easy
    it was?
CACIQUE: You have a powerful god. One minute you
    are one thing, the next, another.
CORTES: We ride horses. The horse is an animal.
    It is a beast of the field that will yield to a man
    on its back.
CITIZENS: Ah! A horse! A horse!
CORTES: We are riding to see Montezuma.
    (Pause. The CACIQUE tightens his lip. The
    CITIZENS go sullen.)
CACIQUE: You will give him horses? Give us horses
    instead. We are your friends.
    (Enter 5 AZTEC TRIBUTE-COLLECTORS,
    richly clad, haughty, holding bunches of flowers
    and followed by attendants with fans. The
    AZTEC TRIBUTE-COLLECTORS talk in
    sequence, phrase by phrase. CORTES exits.)
AZTEC T. C. 1: You must not help
AZTEC T. C. 2: the Easterners without
AZTEC T. C. 3: express permission
AZTEC T. C. 4: from the emperor
AZTEC T. C. 5: Who wants them to

29

AZTEC T. C. 1: go away

CACIQUE (fearfully): We have given them no help!
We are loyal to the emperor Montezuma! The
people of Cempoalla, the nation of the Totonac,
obey the emperor's word!

AZTEC T. C. 1: The emperor has heard

AZTEC T. C. 2: that you are prepared

AZTEC T. C. 3: to revolt against him.

AZTEC T. C. 4: We demand a tribute of twenty

AZTEC T. C. 5: young men and women for sacrifice.

CACIQUE: We are a poor city. You take the best of
our youth for the altars of Tenochtitlan. The
gods are not that hungry.

(Re-enter CORTES.)

CORTES (to CACIQUE): Put them in prison.

CACIQUE: The emperor's tribute-collectors?

CORTES: What right has he to demand the lives of
your people? What a barbarian he must be!
Human sacrifice is the worst crime in the world.
Hasn't anybody told you?

CACIQUE (to the CITIZENS): What do you say?

CITIZENS: Lock them up! Away! Away!

(The TRIBUTE-COLLECTORS are grabbed, and
their attendants.)

AZTEC T. C. 1: Oooh! You'll

AZTEC T. C. 2: Aaah! never

AZTEC T. C. 3: Groo! get

AZTEC T. C. 4: Aieee! away

AZTEC T. C. 5: Help! with this!

30

(The TRIBUTE-COLLECTORS are bundled off. Lights down. Moon up. CORTES exits, then re-appears, wiping his sword, followed by 3 TRIBUTE-COLLECTORS.)

CORTES: There we are. I arranged your release.

AZTEC T. C. 1: We are grateful.

AZTEC T. C. 2: but for your timely

AZTEC T. C. 3: intervention

AZTEC T. C. 1: these treacherous Totonacs

AZTEC T. C. 2: would have surely killed us.

(Enter CACIQUE. Noises off, CITIZENS in an uproar.)

CACIQUE: So you're still here!

CORTES: I caught them trying to escape.

CACIQUE: They murdered the guards! Now we will sacrifice them!

CORTES: They are my prisoners now. I abhor human sacrifice.

CACIQUE: Then may we sacrifice the two that we have got left still in prison? That would be a reasonable compromise.

AZTEC T. C. 1: We must protest

AZTEC T. C. 2: in the strongest possible terms

AZTEC T. C. 3: about the way we are

AZTEC T. C. 1: being used as pawns

AZTEC T. C. 2: in a political game.

CORTES: If you will release the Tribute-Collectors into my care I will return them to the emperor and ask for your nation to be allowed to govern

31

itself as a sovereign state. Montezuma will
listen to me. With my arms, my armour and my
horses, I will be your spokesman and your ally.
I will buy your road to Freedom.
(Exit CORTES with the TRIBUTE-COLLECTORS
(1, 2, 3). The CACIQUE remains behind, scratch-
ing his head.)

CACIQUE: Perhaps it is me that is the beast of
burden? Am I a horse? Who is riding me to
Montezuma?
(CACIQUE exits. GENERAL CROOK sits down
on his camp-stool.)

GENERAL CROOK: Cortes then climbed to the high
plateau of Mexico and fought the Tascalan nation,
with steel and words, until they became horses
too and agreed to help Cortes overthrow the
Aztec. Human sacrifice had to be stamped out.

CRAZY HORSE (laughing): How many men are you,
Gray Wolf? You speak twice for every one word.
Human sacrifice!

GENERAL CROOK: You Indians practised every
damned perversion in the book. Cannibalism!
The Iroquois ate their enemies for strength!

CRAZY HORSE: Who ate Jesus for strength? Ha!

GENERAL CROOK: That was our religion.

CRAZY HORSE: Does that make it better?

GENERAL CROOK: The Apache were the cruellest
torturers I've ever encountered. God, the things
they did to their victims turned my guts up!

32

CRAZY HORSE: They learned well from the Spaniards. The Spaniards taught them to fight fire with fire.

GENERAL CROOK: Slavery, you say. You Indians had slaves!

CRAZY HORSE: Prisoners of war.

GENERAL CROOK: Pah! Women and children? Prisoners of war?

CRAZY HORSE: We never paid gold for men. No Indian ever bought a man.

GENERAL CROOK: You never had any gold. You hadn't got the goddamned sense to dig up what was on your own doorstep!

CRAZY HORSE: Gold was part of the earth, Gray Wolf. It was not the whole meaning of the earth as it was with your people.

(CRAZY HORSE tightens his lip and stares at the floor, then looks up.)

Then the people of Cholula, a city of twenty thousand buildings, asked Cortes to visit them. Like the Totonacs they were tired of Montezuma's tyranny and wanted a treaty with the powerful Spaniard. Cortes came.

(The HEADMEN OF CHOLULA enter from all sides except the aisle. They are unarmed. As they enter they sing.)

HEADMEN OF CHOLULA:

> We have heard of the black powder! Ha!
> We have heard of the hair on the face! Ha!
> Like the black thunder-cloud from the East.

33

We have heard the white man coming.

(CORTES enters with his TWO CONQUISTADORS from the rear of the auditorium and marches up to the HEADMEN OF CHOLULA. The TWO CONQUISTADORS cover the stage R and L exits. The HEADMEN admire their guns, swords and armour and try to touch them. The TWO CON-QUISTADORS fend them off.

CORTES mounts the upper level, then herds all the HEADMEN OF CHOLULA on to the lower level.)

CORTES: Give me room! Give me space! The air stinks! Stand back! I have a man to talk to you! Listen to him well!

HEADMEN OF CHOLULA:

We came to see the horse!

We came to see the strong metal!

We came to be free!

(Enter PRIEST, a Jesuit in black.)

CORTES: Here is the man to make you free!

HEADMEN OF CHOLULA:

We have heard of the black white

And the grey words of his mouth!

We are here for arms, not tongues!

(The HEADMEN OF CHOLULA start to leave but they are stopped by the TWO CONQUIST-ADORS. They retreat, grumbling.)

PRIEST: I have come here to point out the Truth. It is not in your emperor. It is not in your gods.

34

The Truth lies in the god we have found. His
way is the way of love and vengeance, Heaven
and Hell. He is three in one and one in three.

HEADMAN 1: This man talks like the emperor!

HEADMAN 2: Goodbye!

HEADMAN 3: Hello!

PRIEST (angrily): The punishment of sin is Hell and
the heathen lives in a state of perpetual sin. His
foot contaminates the earth he walks upon, his
breath pollutes the air he breathes. His life is a
poisoned river! You must turn to Christ to be
saved. Your souls are in peril. You are tinder
too near the flame!

HEADMEN OF CHOLULA: Take the crow away! Fly
to another tree! No more talk! We have gods!
Our gods understand us!

CORTES: Quiet! This is a man of God, an ordained
priest! You must respect him!

PRIEST: If you would have God's mercy, then be
baptised by me. All those who would enter the
Kingdom of Heaven, come up to me and I will
open the gate! Hear the call! Do not rot in your
heathen ways! God beckons you!
(The PRIEST opens his arms. The HEADMEN
OF CHOLULA do not respond. Silence. CORTES
fumes. He looks meaningly at the TWO CON-
QUISTADORS, who level their arquebuses at the
HEADMEN.)
You are unclean and I offer you water. I am the

35

spiritual power of the East and I carry mercy
in my bag. Give me a chance to save you. If
you reject my word, then the power of the
temporal world must have you. I must hand you
over to the brush to be swept away. This is
your last chance to live. Take it! (Silence. The
PRIEST glares wildly at the HEADMEN.) Then
perish and be damned!

(Blackout. Explosions all round the stage and
auditorium. Screams, mayhem. Five seconds
of noisy, earsplitting chaos. Then silence again.
Lights up. The HEADMEN OF CHOLULA lie
heaped on the lower level, one on top of the
other. CORTES and the TWO CONQUISTADORS
lean on their swords, exhausted with slaughter.)

CORTES: We have done great work for God. There
will be no more human sacrifice here.

PRIEST: God's will is done.

(As GENERAL CROOK and CRAZY HORSE take
up the story, the HEADMEN OF CHOLULA get
up and slip away, followed by CORTES, the
PRIEST and the TWO CONQUISTADORS. Lights
dim as they go, the moon shines again.)

GENERAL CROOK: So Cortes went on from victory
to victory, sweeping all before him. His allies
multiplied daily as his reputation spread.

CRAZY HORSE: He galloped on towards Montezuma's
capital astride the new American horse, civil
war. There the emperor, the man who had

given Cortes pennies to go away like a bad
musician, was forced to yield up his power and
his gold.

GENERAL CROOK: Montezuma stood on one of the
great Aztec pyramids and looked down on his
capital . . .

(Enter MONTEZUMA and stands centre upper-
level. CORTES enters at the rear of the auditorium and mimes the climbing of a giant
pyramid, step by step, the TWO CONQUIST-
ADORS behind him.)

CONQUISTADOR 1 (looking up at MONTEZUMA):
Who does he think he is?

CONQUISTADOR 2: Old Cortes will soon bring him
down to earth.

CONQUISTADOR 1: By the Virgin, they could build.
But they can't fight, eh? So he's the one close to
the gods.

CONQUISTADOR 2: He'll soon be closer than he
thinks.

MONTEZUMA: I am happy to see you. Welcome.
Thank you kindly for laying waste my empire,
stirring up insurrection and civil war, mass-
acring my people and looting my treasuries. I
really am most grateful. I hope you are not
finding the ascent painful?

CORTES (panting): Surrender!

MONTEZUMA: Pause, look about you, there is
Mexico. It is not yours.

CORTES: You are my prisoner.

MONTEZUMA: I am free. (CORTES reaches the top of the pyramid. MONTEZUMA holds out his wrists for a chain). And you do not exist. You are where you came from, across the Eastern Sea. You will not put my city to the sword, you will not murder me. Everything is wonderful. I declare before my gods, there is not a happier man alive than Montezuma. (Pause. MONTE-ZUMA sees Mexico as it is for the first time, the scales fall from his eyes.) Goodbye.

(The TWO CONQUISTADORS lead MONTEZUMA off R. CORTES stands, hands on hips, surveying the world he has won.)

CORTES: I have done it. I, I, I. This is mine!

(The PRIEST pokes his head around the map.)

PRIEST: And mine, brother-in-Christ.

(CORTES exits. Lights dim. Spots on GENERAL CROOK and CRAZY HORSE.)

GENERAL CROOK: The Campaign was over. Mexico became New Spain and a part of the Spanish Empire. As a war of conquest it was a tremen-dous example to future strategists and thinkers specialising in the military arts. Divide and rule. Go for the top. Advance, advance. Be audacious. Arms make the man. Surprise. Terrify. Destroy to build again.

CRAZY HORSE: The disease worse than smallpox was with us.

38

GENERAL CROOK: The new leader of America. Not
        emperors, not kings, not aristocrats, but the
        supreme individualist, the figure head of Free
        Enterprise.
CRAZY HORSE: It was not over. Far to the south
        where The People had drifted there was another
        empire.
GENERAL CROOK (mounting the upper level. Spot
        on map): Here (He points with his sabre) in
        what is now Peru, the Inca ruled five million
        of his subjects much as Montezuma had once
        ruled his.
CRAZY HORSE: With one difference. This Inca was
        not only a great man, but he was also god. He
        had learnt the ways of the white man before he
        had seen them. He was the Sun, he warmed the
        earth.
GENERAL CROOK: The administration of the Inca
        empire was unparalleled. They were the Romans
        of the Americas.
CRAZY HORSE: The Inca empire had survived three
        hundred years, built great cities, roads, a
        government never to be seen again in South
        America. As slaves of the Sun, the Incas were
        the freest men on Earth.
        (GENERAL CROOK sheathes his sabre and
        returns to his alcove. Great burst of light. Crash
        of cymbals, roar of drums, trumpets blow. A
        golden litter with drawn curtains enters from

the rear of the auditorium, carried by BEARERS.
As the BEARERS carry the litter down the aisle
they shout:)

BEARERS: MOST HIGH LORD!

CHILD AND FATHER OF THE SUN!
OUR SOLE AND BELOVED LORD!
SHINE ON! SHINE ON!

CRAZY HORSE: Ten years after the conquest of
Mexico, the Sun himself, the holy Inca, was in
danger. Through the Andes came 117 Spanish
soldiers led by an unlettered criminal, Pizarro.
They were looking for gold, the colour of the
Sun.

(Enter PIZARRO and TWO CONQUISTADORS
stage L, as if climbing a mountain. The INCA'S
litter is carried forward slowly, the BEARERS
chanting. PIZARRO and the TWO CONQUIST-
ADORS reach the top of the mountain and sit
down, looking across to the litter.)

PIZARRO: He is coming!

CRAZY HORSE: From the time that they began their
advance into the Inca's Kingdom Pizarro and
his men had received nothing but hospitality.
They could have been wiped out at any time but
the Inca treated them like honoured guests. It
was the story of the Tainos all over again.

GENERAL CROOK: The Inca was staying at Caxa-
malca and agreed to leave the city to visit
Pizarro in his camp. With the heads of his

40

government and thousands of his followers . . .

CRAZY HORSE: All unarmed . . .

GENERAL CROOK: The Inca entered the Spanish
expedition's quarters.

(PIZARRO and the TWO CONQUISTADORS
mime running down the mountain and go out.
The INCA arrives at the upper level of the stage
and the litter is put down. The INCA remains in
the litter with the curtains drawn. PIZARRO
and the TWO CONQUISTADORS are seen hiding,
armed, stage L and R. FRIAR DE VALVERDE
(who should be in brown, but played by the same
actor as plays the priest) enters stage R with a
Bible.)

BEARERS: We have brought you the Sun.

We have brought you the summer.

FRIAR DE VALVERDE: I don't want to hear your
blasphemies! Uncover him! Let me see the face
of the Devil!

BEARERS: We have brought you the Sun.

We have brought you the summer.

FRIAR DE VALVERDE: In the name of the Pope and
the King of Spain show me this creature! Or is
your litter empty?

(The curtains are pulled back and the INCA
ATAHUALLPA steps out. FRIAR DE VALVERDE
holds out a hand as if to keep the INCA in the
litter.)

FRIAR DE VALVERDE: Back, Satan! Do not stand

like a man of good heart! Your empire is
confiscated by the Holy Catholic Church and
his Catholic Majesty of Spain! I demand that
you be baptised and abjure your ancient evil
faith! Accept Christ and be humble!

(FRIAR DE VALVERDE thrusts the Bible into
the INCA'S hands.)

Say after me, with your hand on this holy book . .
I swear to agree to the annexation of my empire
to that of the Spanish king, and the souls of my
people to the Church of Rome . . .

(The INCA throws the book down.)

INCA: Are you so simple? You stand in the midst of
my country and talk like a child and expect me
to listen? Where is the man I came to see?

FRIAR DE VALVERDE (to PIZARRO): We are wasting
our breath talking to this dog, full of pride as he
is:

(PIZARRO waves a white scarf. Blackout.
Cannon. Gunfire. Confusion. In the darkness
PIZARRO can be heard shouting:)

PIZARRO: Lunge! Detach! Lunge! Detach! Lunge!
Detach!

(Lights up. The BEARERS are in a heap. The
INCA in chains. PIZARRO gets in the litter and
the TWO CONQUISTADORS carry him off, the
INCA following behind like a roped horse.)

GENERAL CROOK: The Incas failed because they had
forgotten the use of arms. 117 men against five

42

million!

CRAZY HORSE: Treachery is a great ally, Gray
Wolf. The white man from the East always had
that regiment on his side. How do you fight
ambition? How do you defeat greed? How do you
turn the flank of deceit or charge the Lie?
Treachery is an army of millions! The cold,
calculating heart is a fortress that no cannon
can breach.

GENERAL CROOK: Soon the wealth of Peru was
flooding back across the Atlantic to Spain to
support her continental empire. Spain had
become the most powerful nation on earth. The
gold of America bought her the fear of the
civilised world.

CRAZY HORSE: And the New World
              Was made old
                  by gold.
(GENERAL CROOK about-turns, salutes the flag,
then marches off R. CRAZY HORSE sits by the
BEARERS and starts to sing a mourning-song.)
          The People, where are the People?
          Where are the Tainos now?
          Where are the Arawaks?
          Where are the Aztecs?
          Where are the Incas?
          The People, where are the People?
(Lights darken. The wind rises. The huddled,
blanketed figures enter from the rear of the

43

auditorium. The BEARERS slowly rise. They
all join CRAZY HORSE in the chant, louder and
louder. The people are everywhere in the theatre,
singing.)

> The People, where are the People?
> Where are the Tainos now?
> Where are the Arawaks?
> Where are the Aztecs?
> Where are the Incas?
> The People, where are the People?

(The moon is illuminated. As the chant continues, over and over, GENERAL CROOK enters
with a bucket of whitewash and a brush and care-
fully paints in the Caribbean, Mexico, Honduras,
Peru. The paint should run into the adjoining
countries. When he has finished he exits and
the people fade away, leaving the auditorium
empty.)

ACT TWO

Thudding of a drum. Bugle call. Enter GENERAL
CROOK and CRAZY HORSE to their places.
    The pianist plays a selected piece by Claude le
Jeune (or another French composer of the period).
After a bar, the fleur-de-lys is carried in from the
rear of the auditorium by JACQUES CARTIER. He
marches down the aisle, stabs at the St. Lawrence
valley . . . plants the flag.

CARTIER: Here! I claim these lands on behalf of
    King Francis the First of France!
CRAZY HORSE: The Iroquois held that land from
    the Master of Life. It was theirs.
    (The pianist plays a selected piece by William
    Byrd. The Royal Standard of Elizabeth I is
    carried down the aisle by SIR WALTER RAL-
    EIGH. He prods the coast of South Carolina . . .
    plants the flag.)
SIR WALTER RALEIGH: Here! I claim these lands
    on behalf of Queen Elizabeth of England!
CRAZY HORSE: The Santee Sioux held that land from
    the Great Spirit. It was theirs.

(The pianist plays a selected piece by Sweelinck
(or any other Dutch composer of the early 17th
century), and the flag of the Netherlands is
carried in by PETER MINUIT. He points at
Manhattan Island . . . plants the flag.)

PETER MINUIT: Here! I claim these lands on
behalf of the States General and the Dutch West
India Company!

CRAZY HORSE: But here it wasn't so easy. A
passing band of Indians overheard . . .
(TWO INDIANS (the tribe is not known) appear
from behind the map of America. They wag
their fingers at PETER MINUIT, then hold out
their hands.)

INDIAN A: One hundred dollars!.

PETER MINUIT: I'll give you five!

INDIAN B: Seventy dollars!

PETER MINUIT: I'll give you ten!

INDIAN A: Fifty dollars!

PETER MINUIT: I'll give you fifteen!

INDIAN B: Forty dollars!

PETER MINUIT: I'll give you twenty!
(The TWO INDIANS nod. They all shake hands.
PETER MINUIT produces a piece of parchment
and a pen. He spreads it out on the floor. The
TWO INDIANS start singing and dance all over
the paper. PETER MINUIT shoves them off and
waves the pen under their noses.)

PETER MINUIT: Sign! Sign!

(INDIAN A takes the quill off MINUIT, looks at
it, then sticks it in his hair and carries on
dancing. MINUIT grabs the quill and bends down
over the parchment, showing them how to sign.
The TWO INDIANS play leapfrog over his back.)

MINUIT: Sign! Sign, you damned savages!

(The TWO INDIANS kneel down by MINUIT'S
side. He gives INDIAN A the quill. INDIAN A
gives it to INDIAN B, who gives it back again.
MINUIT gives it to INDIAN B, who gives it to
INDIAN A, who gives it back again. Then both
INDIANS put their hands together and pray.)

INDIAN A: O Great Spirit, guide our hands!

INDIAN B: For we cannot write!

MINUIT: Then make your mark!

(The TWO INDIANS make their marks, shake
hands with MINUIT, receive their 20 dollars in
coin.)

MINUIT: That's settled that! Now the island is mine!
Not bad for twenty dollars, eh?

INDIAN A: You got a bargain.

INDIAN B: But now we must be going home.

MINUIT: Wait a minute. You can't live here any
more. This place is mine.

INDIAN A: We never lived here in the first place. We
are just passing through.

(The TWO INDIANS run off. MINUIT chases
them, then comes back, takes up the parchment
as if to tear it, pauses, shrugs, then rolls it up

47

and puts it back in his shirt.)

MINUIT: It will have to do.

GENERAL CROOK: And thus began the legend of the
"Honest Injun".

(The 3 Colonisers - French, English and Dutch -
stand with their flags. Sounds of wind, sea, the
screams of gulls. Enter 3 groups through the
auditorium, carrying poles on which sails are
raised (in the way a trade union banner is
carried).)

GENERAL CROOK: The Atlantic Ocean was bridged
more often than the Seine, the Thames or the
Zuyder Zee.

CRAZY HORSE: And they brought a different god,
for they were rebels against the Spanish way.
There was no talk of the great chief in Rome.
Their god was in a book and they brought him
in libraries of Bibles, they sailed on Bibles . . .

GENERAL CROOK: Puritans from England, Huguen-
ots from France, Calvinists from the Netherlands,
they came to plant the orchards of their faith as
well as their apples. Europe was once again in
the hands of Rome and they went to America,
preferring a Devil they did not know to a Devil
they knew.

(The 3 ships sail slowly towards the upper
level. The EMIGRANTS pray together in a
spoken chorus.)

EMIGRANTS: Sail with us, O Lord,

48

For you were a sailor,
You walked upon the water
As these wooden shoes of ships
Tread the waves:
Protect us from the unknown
Depths of this mighty sea,
Protect us from the heathen
And the ways of darkness,
And on land, as on sea,
Keep us close to Thee.
Amen. Amen. Amen.

(The ships reach the upper level. The EMI-
GRANTS land, carrying axes, ropes, guns,
spades. They cluster round the flags. Sound
effects of axes biting into wood, trees crashing,
spades turning earth. The EMIGRANTS mime
with the sounds, building, building, working,
working. The sounds get louder and louder, the
EMIGRANTS work faster and faster until the
sound is deafening and the EMIGRANTS are
moving at frenzied speed. The TWO INDIANS
(A & B) enter on the upper level and watch,
shaking their heads in wonder. They carry
baskets of fruit, corn, vegetables. The EMI-
GRANTS work on. The TWO INDIANS shrug and
go out, leaving the baskets behind. Sounds stop
abruptly. The EMIGRANTS drop to the ground
with exhaustion and sleep. Lights down. Night.)
GENERAL CROOK: Their god was Work, their

Christ, industry. For a man to pay his way in
the world was salvation started. They bored
into America like beetles.

CRAZY HORSE: They felled our forests, polluted
our streams, slew our game and scorned our
ways. Like fools, the Indian gave the beetle
food, helped him with his burrowing.

(Sound of feet marching, tramping, hundreds
of boots, an army, tramp! tramp! As the moon
shines on and the EMIGRANTS sleep, the tramping grows louder. At its zenith there is a loud
yell, the lights go up and METACOMET, Chief
of the Wampanoags, leaps onstage in full war-
paint, armed, wearing a golden crown.)

METACOMET: Enough, Yinglees! Enough Yinglees!
Out! Out! Damn Yankees!

(The FLAG-BEARERS and the EMIGRANTS
retreat to the lower level in confusion. The
Dutch and French flags are placed alongside the
Stars and Stripes, the English remains. META-
COMET takes the crown off and throws it into
the midst of the EMIGRANTS.)

METACOMET: Take this hat away you gave me!
Tell the White Father over the Eastern Sea that
it is heavy and hollow: . . .

EMIGRANT 1: But, King Philip . . .

METACOMET: You flatter me with an empty title!
You duped my father into thinking that he ruled
his own house while it was you who governed

50

my people! I am not a king! Nor is your king a
king here! You are going home, back to where
you came from!

(Enter 4 WAMPANOAGS in full war-paint with
bows. They line up behind METACOMET.)

METACOMET: Go away! Go back to England! Take
your god, your books, and your guns and go! We
had peace in this land until the Trickster spirits
brought you to torment us! Metacomet speaks!
Out! Out!

(The EMIGRANTS murmur and brace themselves into a line. The WAMPANOAGS mime
the firing of arrows, the EMIGRANTS mime
the firing of guns. Slowly the EMIGRANTS
advance, the WAMPANOAGS drop one by one
until only METACOMET is left. Pause. META-
COMET backs away, faced by the hostile eyes
of the EMIGRANTS.)

METACOMET: Where is King Philip now? Where is
your slave?

(He throws himself at the EMIGRANTS. They
seize him and he goes down under a milling
heap of fists and boots. Blackout. Two spots on
GENERAL CROOK and CRAZY HORSE. The
stage is cleared. The English flag is put with
the Stars and Stripes.)

GENERAL CROOK: In a campaign remarkable for
its ferocity, King Philip was defeated. The
settlers looked upon his attempt to drive them

51

out of their homes as a betrayal. Had the
Indian not been baptised, educated in an English
school?

CRAZY HORSE: Metacomet had the right idea. He
was the first Indian chief to see the danger and
the first to try and create an alliance against
the whites. He brought the Narragansets of
Rhode Island, the Pequots of Connecticut, and
other small tribes into a common cause against
the invaders. He saw the way to beat them back
into the sea.

GENERAL CROOK: King Philip lost his war. He was
caught and hacked to bits and his wife and child
sold into slavery. He had been outgunned and
outgeneralled.

CRAZY HORSE: And the tribes of the alliance
perished. They were no more, like snow in
summer. Now we can add to my song.
(A drum starts up, soft rattle. CRAZY HORSE
takes up his chant again:)

> The People, where are the People?
> Where are the Tainos now?
> Where are the Arawaks?
> Where are the Aztecs?
> Where are the Incas?
> Where are the Wampanoags?
> Where are the Pequots?
> Where are the Narragansets?
> Where are the People?

GENERAL CROOK (pointing with his sabre on the
    map): For the next two centuries the European
    colonists moved inland through the passes of
    the Allegheny Mountains and down the westward-
    flowing rivers of the Mississippi . . .
CRAZY HORSE (bitterly): The Great Waters!
GENERAL CROOK: And then up the Missouri . . .
CRAZY HORSE: The Great Muddy!
GENERAL CROOK: Various chiefs tried to do what
    King Philip . . .
CRAZY HORSE: The hero Metacomet!
GENERAL CROOK: . . . had tried to do. Pontiac of
    the Ottawas united the tribes of the Great Lakes
    to drive the British back over the Allegheny
    Mountains in 1760. He failed because he made
    a fatal error - he brought the French into the
    alliance - there was war in Europe . . . the
    British and the French . . .
CRAZY HORSE: There was always war in Europe!
GENERAL CROOK: And the French broke faith with
    the peaux-rouges, their Indian allies, at the
    siege of Detroit. The Ottawas were crushed.
CRAZY HORSE: Where are the Ottawas? Trusting a
    white man? What innocence!
GENERAL CROOK: Fifty years later Tecumseh of
    the Shawnees formed a confederacy of mid-
    western tribes to protect their homelands from
    the British, Dutch, French, German, Spanish
    invaders. The Scramble for America was on!

53

CRAZY HORSE: Tecumseh died in battle, his dream died with him.

GENERAL CROOK: For the first half of the nine-teenth-century the Miamis of the fertile Ohio valley fought battle after battle . . .

CRAZY HORSE: Signed treaty after treaty . . .

GENERAL CROOK: Until there was nothing left of their land to cede.

CRAZY HORSE: Miami, Miami . . . do you know the word?

GENERAL CROOK: Black Hawk of the Foxes refused to hand over his tribal lands to the white settlers after the white man's war of 1812, when the Americans fought the -

CRAZY HORSE: Notice the name - Americans! Americans! We were the Americans!

GENERAL CROOK: By then the Revolution of 1776 was ancient history, Crazy Horse! We licked the British hands down, all ways up! We declared our independence . . .

CRAZY HORSE: Yes, your independence! What about ours? We were the first Americans! We had a right to be consulted!

GENERAL CROOK: Let's get back to Black Hawk. He was quite a soldier.

CRAZY HORSE: America arrived without the Red Indian even knowing about it. Out of the white men's wars came a paper, a name, another army. The United States. Europe was inside us.

(GENERAL CROOK stands to attention and
salutes. The pianist plays "The Stars and
Stripes". CRAZY HORSE holds his head in his
hands.)

CRAZY HORSE: And then they started stirring the
pot again. They had sold The People into slavery
for two hundred years, now they went to Africa
and bought slaves to bring to America - black
slaves, for they were fast running out of red as
blood runs out of an opened vein.
(Slow fade to darkness. Chinking of chains.
Blackout. Chinking of chains becomes rhythmical
as the voices of the SLAVES sing the slave-song.)

SLAVES: You cannot see us
               because of the darkness,
               you cannot hold us
               because of the night,
               we are black in the blackness
               and blue in the blueness
               of the sea and the bruise
               in our hearts.
               Hahe! (The chains crash) Hahe!
               Only Death sets us free!

(Sounds of the ships again, creaking of timbers,
stretching of yards. The chinking of chains continues in rhythm. Blackout continues, complete
darkness.)

               We are sold to work sugar,
               we are sold to work cotton,

55

            we are sold to be horses
            and our manhood forgotten!
            We die on the coast,
            we die in the hold,
            we live to be bought
            with American gold!
            Hahe! (The chains crash) Hahe!
            Only death sets us free.
    (Ships' sounds fade. Hammering on a block.
    Murmur of a crowd. Blackout remains.)
AUCTIONEER: Now what am I bid?
SLAVES: I'm ten! I'm five! I'm twelve! I'm alive!
            Bid in dollars or gold,
            I'm here to be sold!
    (Crash of the AUCTIONEER'S hammer.)
GENERAL CROOK: The Indian would not work! He
    had never learned to work! The routine of your
    lives was idleness!
CRAZY HORSE: They brought the black men in
    thousands to work the fields of a plant that
    could not be eaten.
GENERAL CROOK: Cotton, the mainstay of the
    American export trade with the Old Country.
CRAZY HORSE: We were being conquered by the
    price of a thin shirt. Where the black men came
    in, we were pushed out . . .
GENERAL CROOK: We were a young, vigorous,
    expanding country. We needed room! People
    came to America for a new life, to be free to

56

live in peace, to worship the god of their choice . . .

CRAZY HORSE: Gold.

GENERAL CROOK: Dammit, Crazy Horse, gold to
the white man was only a means to an end. Our
economy was based on gold. We had to have it.
(Enter stage L the FRENCH ESTATE AGENT.
He is dressed in top hat, coat and breeches and
carries a cane.)

FRENCH ESTATE AGENT: M'sieur! Psst! Psst!
A word in your ear!

GENERAL CROOK: Who's this goddamned dandy?

FRENCH ESTATE AGENT (sidling over to CROOK):
'Ere, 'ow would you like to buy a piece of
America? You like?
(The FRENCH ESTATE AGENT takes out a
sheaf of post-cards and sticks them under
CROOK'S nose.)

FRENCH ESTATE AGENT: Voila! Is she not lovely?

GENERAL CROOK: That's New Orleans! What the
hell's going on here?

FRENCH ESTATE AGENT: 'Ere is the Mississippi,
the Red River, is Louisiana not beautiful, eh?
You can have 'er, for the right price, of course.
You like what you see?

CRAZY HORSE: Ask him about sitting tenants.

GENERAL CROOK (to FRENCH ESTATE AGENT):
You heard him. What about sitting tenants?

FRENCH ESTATE AGENT: Take no notice of 'im.
He is a peau-rouge. Listen, my friend, the

French people are willing to sell you this des-
irable property with magnificent views over the
Gulf of Mexico for a mere 15, 000, 000 dollars -

CRAZY HORSE: Ask him about the chattels, then. Do
they go with the property? Do you get the
Chitimichas, the Taenzas, the Natchez, the
Karoks, the Yazoos, the Choctaws and the
Chickasaws thrown in?

GENERAL CROOK: Well, Crazy Horse, it sounds a
bargain. It's a better way of acquiring territory
than war. (To the FRENCH ESTATE AGENT) I
reckon if you go and see the President in Washington he'll be interested.

FRENCH ESTATE AGENT: Merci bien. Au revoir.
(The FRENCH ESTATE AGENT exits after a
courtly bow and a wave of his stick.)

CRAZY HORSE: And that is how it was done. The
white man had come to America for gold, he
got gold, and with that gold he now started
buying the land off people who didn't even own
it. The earth was bought and sold from under
The People's feet. In 1803 the Great White
Father bought Louisiana.
(Enter stage L a MEXICAN GENERAL. He is in
military uniform and so loaded with medals that
he leans over to one side.)

MEXICAN GENERAL: Hey, damn Yankee, c'm 'ere,
I gotta someting to tell you.

GENERAL CROOK: What do you want, you damn
58

greaser?

MEXICAN GENERAL: Now we don' like da war, eh?
What is da point of it all? We are neighbours.
Now, I'll do you a deal, a nice deal. The Mexican government, well, we don' wanna get in
your hairs, eh? Like you say, we like to keep
it peaceful.

GENERAL CROOK: Speak up then, Mex. We've
trounced you all over the place lately. What's
the deal?

MEXICAN GENERAL: You remember the deal you
did with the Spanish government in 1813?

GENERAL CROOK: Yes, we bought West Florida
from them after the war.

CRAZY HORSE: The squatters at that time were the
Bilox, the Seminoles, the Apalachee. What
rights had they got in these dealings? They had
only lived there for ten thousand years.

MEXICAN GENERAL: Well, if I remember right,
you paid 5, 000, 000 dollars for that piece of land.

GENERAL CROCK: That's right.

MEXICAN GENERAL: How much you give for California, Utah, Texas and New Mexico?
(Pause: GENERAL CROOK scratches his head.)

GENERAL CROCK: Dammit, man, that's a mighty
big parcel of territory.

CRAZY HORSE (angrily facing the MEXICAN
GENERAL): Who says you can sell this land?
It is not yours to sell!

MEXICAN GENERAL: Who is this barbarian? Get
back to your reservation, Indios!

CRAZY HORSE: You brought your wars to our land
and you sought to settle them with our land and
our gold. Who are you to put the earth on the
market? Are you God? You have enough medals
for God but inside you are a cheap swindler.
You cannot sell what is not yours!

MEXICAN GENERAL: Yankee, don't listen to this
ignorant savage. He is talking nonsense. You
and me are men of the world, eh? What will
you offer me? These places are like Paradise
on earth.

CRAZY HORSE: What about the Apaches?

MEXICAN GENERAL: Apaches! (Spits on the ground)
Fiends from Hell! They are no better than
rattlesnake! The gringos can have the Apaches
and the Modocs, the Mohaves, the Paiutes,
the Shastas, the Yumas, the Navahoes and the
Utes. Because of this little disadvantage I am
only asking for 15, 000, 000 dollars. Without the
Indians, well, I think I ask for 25, 000, 000.

GENERAL CROOK: That's a fair offer, Mex. If I
was you I'd go and have talk with the President.
I know he thinks that we should get our border
down on to the Rio Grande.
(The MEXICAN GENERAL salutes, then exits.
CRAZY HORSE returns to his alcove and squats
on his blanket.)

GENERAL CROOK: In 1844 the Mexican government
sold Texas, California, Utah and New Mexico
to the United States for 15, 000, 000 dollars. We
were across to the West coast!
(GENERAL CROOK marches off and gets the
whitewash and brush. He paints in all the territory west of 95° longitude, then sweeps round
through Texas, New Mexico, to Utah as CRAZY
HORSE sings his mourning song, accompanied
by drum and rattles.)

CRAZY HORSE: Where are the People?
Where are the Chitimichas?
Where are the Taenzas?
Where are the Natchez?
Where are the Karoks?
Where are the Yazoos?
Where are the Choctaws?
Where are the Chickasaws?
Where are the Bilox?
Where are the Apalachees?
Where are the Seminoles?
Where are the Apaches?
Where are the Modocs?
Where are the Mohaves?
Where are the Paiutes?
Where are the Shastas?
Where are the Yumas?
Where are the Navahoes?
Where are the Utes?

(GENERAL CROOK puts away the whitewash and
returns to his alcove. CRAZY HORSE sits with
his head in his hands.)

CRAZY HORSE: Remember Sharp Knife? (stands up
and goes to map)

GENERAL CROOK: You mean Andrew Jackson? A
damn fine soldier, and President of the United
States . . .

CRAZY HORSE: As well as the killer of thousands of
Cherokees, Chickasaws, Choctaws, Creeks and
Seminoles.

GENERAL CROOK: Dammit, man, he was a soldier.
He fought you Indians because it was his duty.

CRAZY HORSE: A soldier is a man of honour?

GENERAL CROOK: His honour is his life.

CRAZY HORSE: Then why did Sharp Knife say in 1829
that this was the Permanent Indian Frontier?
This line, the course of the Great Waters, the
Mississippi, was to be the wall I wanted. Beyond
it no white man could go. That was the law he
made through your Congress. It was written
down! He promised that we should have all this
land in the West for ourselves. And we - fools
that we were - believed him!

GENERAL CROOK: The war with Mexico changed
everything. The settlers were pouring into
Wisconsin and Iowa, the miners were in Utah
where gold had been found. Jackson couldn't
hold them back.

CRAZY HORSE: Then do not talk to me of laws and
        peace! Sharp Knife allowed his white children
        to break all the rules and they were never
        punished. Only the Indians died.
GENERAL CROOK: Minnesota became a state, its
        frontier extending a hundred miles beyond the
        second Permanent Indian Frontier.
CRAZY HORSE: The People were in a vice and only
        war could save them.
        (The pianist softly plays "Way Down South in
        Dixie". The tune is taken up by whistling. A
        vaulting horse is dragged on-stage (to the lower
        level). GENERAL CROOK mounts his steed.
        The AUCTIONEER and the NEGRO go out. The
        pianist slides into "The Battle Hymn of the
        Republic". Softly, slowly he plays as GENERAL
        CROOK begins to trot, breaks into a canter,
        then he thunders fortissimo as GENERAL
        CROOK draws his sabre and . . .)
GENERAL CROOK: Charge! Long live the Union!
        (Lights switch to red. GENERAL CROOK slows
        down, he cuts and thrusts with his sabre in
        slow-motion. The pianist picks out both the
        Confederate and Union tunes alternately, then
        fades. GENERAL CROOK is exhausted, slides
        off his horse and pushes it into his alcove.)
CRAZY HORSE: The war that The People thought
        might save them was a white man's war - the
        North versus the South. The white men forgot

63

the red men and fought over the black men. It
was the worst war ever seen in America. When
we saw how the white man fought his friends we
knew what we could expect as his enemies. And
his armies got bigger and bigger, his wagon-
guns longer, his pony soldiers as numerous as
summer flies.

GENERAL CROOK: The United States were preserved
We whipped the rebels and on July 28th 1868
the Fourteenth Amendment became part of the
Constitution. All citizens of the United States
were to have equal rights, black or white . . .

CRAZY HORSE: But not red. The Civil War had not
been fought for us.

(The red light fades and is replaced by the
moon. From every entrance, stage and auditorium, steps an Indian in full war-paint. They
are CHIEFS of the people who fought the United
States Army from 1860 to 1890. They stand
round the stage and auditorium and step a pace
forward as CRAZY HORSE calls out their names.

CRAZY HORSE: These are only the leaders of The
People in those last thirty years. By the time
the whites had shut the door of Freedom in our
faces, The People had been cut in half. We were
not many, maybe three hundred thousand of us
were left. We wanted peace but we were not
ready to take the black man's place. We were
men! We were The People!

Little Crow of the Santee Sioux
Black Kettle of the Southern Cheyennes
Mangas Colorado of the Mimbrenos Apaches
Spotted Tail of the Brules
Satanta of the Kiowas
Quanah Parker of the Comanches
Captain Jack of the Modocs
Joseph of the Nez Perces
Big Foot of the Minneconjous
Standing Bear of the Poncas
Sitting Bull of the Hunkpapa Sioux
Wovoka of the Paiutes

(Pause)

and CRAZY HORSE, The Big Dreamer.
(To the audience) You are now in a familiar
situation. You are surrounded by Indians!
(All the CHIEFS leap in the air and shout. It
must be a clear, sudden sound. Pause.)
CRAZY HORSE: Since the time when I was a boy in
the Black Hills I have been a dreamer, a seeker
after visions. This was never the real world to
me. Even in life I sought after the dream. I
went up into the mountains, I lay on rafts of
wood on hidden lakes for days without food, I
sat under the stars, always I stayed with my
dream. Crazy Horse, the Big Dreamer, was
the dream of The People. I had seen it all from
long ago. From the time we crossed the land-
bridge to this moment, I was in the head of the

65

Great Spirit, peering from behind his eyes. I
saw what would happen to The People but all I
had was my short life, my lance and my horse,
to fight against the whites and what they were
doing. By being born I became just one Indian
and I faced a truth as terrible as my dream.
My dream and the truth were the same thing.
(Pause) MOUNT UP, GENERAL GRAY WOLF
THREE STARS GOD ALMIGHTY!
(CRAZY HORSE runs to the vaulting horse and
drags it out to the centre of the lower level,
pats the leather. As soon as he touches the
leather the CHIEFS scream again and rush towards GENERAL CROOK, lift him up and dump
him on the vaulting-horse. There should be a
moment of nervousness as the CHIEFS descend
on the GENERAL, then relief as he is hoisted
into the air.)

CRAZY HORSE: Now be all our enemies, Gray Wolf!

LITTLE CROW: Be Myrick the trader who told us to
eat grass!

BLACK KETTLE: Be Colonel Chivington who killed
us at Sand Creek!

MANGAS COLORADO: Be Colonel West who broke
his word!

SPOTTED TAIL: Be the white hunters who slaught-
ered the buffalo!

SATANTA: Be General Sheridan who wanted us dead!

QUANAH PARKER: Be Great Warrior Sherman who

66

butchered our horses!

CAPTAIN JACK: Be Commissioner Meacham who
told us the Law was dead!

JOSEPH: Be One-Armed Soldier Howard who drove
us to the ground!

BIG FOOT: Be Colonel Forsyth who killed us in the
snow!

STANDING BEAR: Be Inspector Kemble who took us
to the Quapaw to die!

SITTING BULL: Be Hard Backsides Custer who tried
to break our hearts!

WOVOKA: Be white! Be white!

CRAZY HORSE: Be yourself who came looking for
me in the Cold Moons!

Hopo hook-ahay!

And be the Great White Father in Washington
who turned his back upon his children.

Let's go!

(The pianist plays a steady, monotonous rhythm
of heavy bass chords. Drummers occupy CRAZY
HORSE'S alcove and take up the rhythm. The
CHIEFS return to their previous positions
around stage and auditorium step by step to the
rhythm. GENERAL CROOK sits astride his
horse, looking straight ahead. The pianist hits
the chords again. The drummers drum. LITTLE
CROW comes forward.)

LITTLE CROW: It was my fault. I had signed the
treaties that tricked away our land around the

67

Minnesota River. All we had left was a strip by the waters and the whites were waiting for that. The Santee Sioux were poor. The Santee Sioux were hungry. All we had was our money and our rations from the Great Council in Washington, but in that year they had no money, for the gold was being spent on the war between the Bluecoats and the Graycoats. My people were starving. The rations were in the stores but there was no money. We saw food but could not eat. I went to the trader Myrick . . . (He looks up at GENERAL CROOK.) and I said, "We have waited a long time. Give us food so we do not starve. When the money comes it will be yours." What did he say?

GENERAL CROOK: So far as I'm concerned, if they are hungry let them eat grass or their own dung. (Pause: then GENERAL CROOK slowly slides off his horse and lies down, his mouth open. LITTLE CROW takes a handful of grass out of his shirt and stuffs it into CROOK'S mouth.)

LITTLE CROW: So we made Myrick eat grass himself. Then we fought the soldiers who came. We fought as men and it was the guns that beat us. When we were taken they put us in prison and tried us. The Great White Father Lincoln said 39 of us must hang and hang we did. Those that were left were put in ships to go up the Missouri River to where the soil was barren,

there was no game, and the alkaline water unfit
for drinking. The Santee Sioux were finished.
(GENERAL CROOK spits out the grass and re-
mounts his horse. LITTLE CROW shakes his
head and returns to his place. The pianist
strikes the chords again, the drummers drum.
BLACK KETTLE comes into the spot.)
BLACK KETTLE: I am Cheyenne and I could talk of
massacre and murder, of land stealing, of the
long walks of my people through hard winters
to find a refuge from the pony-soldiers. But I
will not. My story will be one story. It will
show you that we were not perfect, we were
proud. Two boys, Chief-in-Head and Humped
Over, killed a white man who wrongly accused
them of stealing a cow. One cow . . .
(CHIEF-IN-HEAD enter stage R and HUMPED
OVER stage L. CHIEF-IN-HEAD wears a full
eagle-feather war-bonnet. HUMPED OVER a
single feather. They enter and stand still.)
The Army came to the Cheyennes and demanded
these murderers. We did not want war, we were
sick of war, but we could not hand over the boys.
They had gone to the Wolf Mountains. They said
that the white man had deserved to die. Their
fathers went to them and asked that they come
down to the soldiers. They would give them a
fair trial. The boys laughed and said:
CHIEF-IN-HEAD: We have heard of the fair trials.

69

We will not come in.

HUMPED OVER: But tomorrow at noon we will be at this point in the hills.

CHIEF-IN-HEAD: Tell the soldiers to come and get us.

BLACK KETTLE: That night we danced for the boys We sent them two of our best horses, our richest shirts, our finest arms. The boys painted themselves as for the old Sun Dance which the Great Father in Washington had forbidden us to perform, they anointed themselves with oil, and then waited in the noonday sun.

(CHIEF-IN-HEAD and HUMPED OVER should dress and paint themselves as BLACK KETTLE speaks, following the course of the dialogue.)

BLACK KETTLE (to CROOK): Sir, you are two hundred mounted men. The Army of the Great Father sent out three troops of pony soldiers to catch our boys. Ride!

(CROOK salutes, rides, bugle call.)

GENERAL CROOK: Forward!

BLACK KETTLE: The pony soldiers came to the point in the hills. Here the earth was like a bowl and The People were there, all of us, old and young, to see what our boys would do. We heard their singing and knew the sound of it.

CHIEF-IN-HEAD: I will stop growing older.

They will put an end

To my growing!

HUMPED OVER: Watch us while we are riding,

How we ride our horses.

Watch our skill.

(CROOK reins in, then dismounts, takes out his
revolver and stands behind the horse, facing
the upper-level. The BOYS carry on chanting,
then bring down their lances and charge at
CROOK, miming the horses beneath them.
Sound of heavy rifle-fire. The BOYS chant on.
CROOK mimes blazing away at his attackers.
HUMPED OVER drops. CHIEF-IN-HEAD gets
closer, carries through past CROOK and then
drops.)

BLACK KETTLE: Chief-In- Head took six wounds.
He rode through the two hundred men dead, but
still on his horse. Humped Over was not hit bad
and crawled to cover in a dry wash. The soldiers
came for him and he fought well.

GENERAL CROOK (Turning to the audience, for the
first time evidently moved by what has happened):
A young lieutenant found him. These are his
words. "Crawling through the brush towards
him, we suddenly discovered him dead, and we
were most startled at the weird beauty of the
picture he made as he lay in his vivid colour of
costume and painted face, his red blood dyeing
the yellow of autumn leaves on which he fell. "

BLACK KETTLE: That is my story.

71

(BLACK KETTLE returns to his place. CHIEF-
IN-HEAD and HUMPED OVER go out. MANGAS
COLORADO jumps into the spot. Throughout
his account of his betrayal and death he mimes
the action, instructing CROOK when he requires
his help in telling the story. CROOK obeys like
an automaton, showing no feeling, his expression
frozen. He becomes each antagonist for each
CHIEF as they tell their mimed stories. Every
CHIEF addresses the audience throughout.)

MANGAS COLORADO: My people lived in Arizona
and New Mexico, from the Chiricuhua Mountains
to the Mogollons. We tried to stop the white
men coming. In the war between the Bluecoats
and the Graycoats we managed to drive the
Graycoats out into the East. Then came Star
Chief Carleton from California along the old
trail through our mountains. We fought him,
and he suffered at our hands. So they asked for
a truce. Colonel Joseph West (CROOK salutes)
met me at Fort McLean. He made me a prisoner
although I had come under the white flag. That
night he told two soldiers to guard me. He said
to them . . .

GENERAL CROOK: I want him dead or alive tomorrow
morning, do you understand, I want him dead.

MANGAS COLORADO: I lay down to sleep by the
fire under my blanket. The soldiers heated
their bayonets in the fire and put them to the

72

soles of my feet. I endured it until I could take
no more, then I rose and said "I am no child to
be played with in this way." The soldiers
pointed their muskets at me and shot me dead.
(Pause. MANGAS COLORADO looks up at
GENERAL CROOK, who stares straight ahead.
Shaking his head MANGAS COLORADO returns
to his place. CROOK sits still on his horse, his
head hanging. The pianist plays the chords, the
drummers drum. SATANTA, SPOTTED TAIL
and QUANAH PARKER jump forward into the
spot.)

SATANTA: This is how we hunted buffalo, the big
ones.

(Sound effect of cattle lowing and bellowing (a
substitute for buffalo noise). The BUFFALO
enters from rear of auditorium. The four
CHIEFS are armed with lances. The piano
stops and the drums get louder as the four
CHIEFS hunt the BUFFALO, two on either
side, keeping the BUFFALO on a straight
course. The CHIEFS shout at the BUFFALO.
As the hunt progresses round the theatre, the
remaining CHIEFS sing and clap:)

CHIEFS: Ha-hey-ya-hey
            ya-hey-ya-hey-ya-hey
            ha-hey-ya-hey
            ya-hey-ya-hey-ya-hey
            ha-hey-ya-he

ya-hey-ya-hey-ya-hey

ha-hey-ya-he

(The BUFFALO is killed by a lance thrust to
the heart.)

SATANTA (suddenly turning on CROOK): You butcher!
Your belly never needed that much meat!

QUANAH PARKER: In one year the whites killed
four million buffalo.

SPOTTED TAIL: They killed more buffalo than
Indians. They put all their heart into it. They
killed for the coat, for the coat!

SATANTA: Now you are Sheridan. I ask you - sir,
should not something be done to stop the sense-
less killing of the buffalo? What is your answer,
General? What will you do about the white
hunters?

GENERAL CROOK: Let them kill, skin and sell
until the buffalo is exterminated, as it is the
only way to bring lasting peace and allow civilisation to advance.

SATANTA: Starve us to death. Take the meat out of
the mother's mouth. You are children murdering
children. Death is the white man's game.
(CAPTAIN JACK leaps out into the spot, shaking
his fist under CROOK'S nose.)

CAPTAIN JACK: Councils! Councils! Councils! Oh,
councils killed poor Captain Jack! In our valley
there ran enough deer, antelope, duck and fish
for everyone! And where did I end up?

74

(SATANTA, QUANAH PARKER, SPOTTED
TAIL leave the spot, dragging the buffalo.
CAPTAIN JACK continues. He is slightly mad,
very active and full of gestures.)

CAPTAIN JACK: Hear me! This man Canby here
has killed me! I charge him!

GENERAL CROOK: My orders are to move you out
of the Lost River Valley by force if need be.

CAPTAIN JACK (grovelling, in caricature): I will go,
I will take all my people with me. Let me kiss
your boots!

GENERAL CROOK (kicking at CAPTAIN JACK): I'm
not here to make trouble, Captain Jack.

CAPTAIN JACK: You would never make trouble.
Cheat us out of our land, yes. Kill our people,
yes. Set fire to our village, yes. But trouble?
Never. (He clings to GENERAL CROOK'S boots,
smothering them with kisses.)

GENERAL CROOK: Off, you red devil!
(CAPTAIN JACK springs back, his manner
changed.)

CAPTAIN JACK: Then we saw that we were men. We
went to a place where no man can live, the
Lava Beds, where there is nothing but stone.
No grass grows. No birds sing. It is the grave.
We fought the soldiers there and they killed me.
The Modocs were finished. But I had words to
say.
(CAPTAIN JACK runs from place to place,

delivering a sentence at one place, running,
pausing, delivering another. He does this at
top speed. GENERAL CROOK has to strain
round to keep him in view.)

CAPTAIN JACK: I am but one man. (move)

I am the voice of my people. (move)

I am not afraid to die. (move)

I have come to these rocks to
fight. (move)

I have a red skin. (move)

I have red blood. (move)

I have one heart. (move)

(CAPTAIN JACK stands still, pointing at his
heart. CROOK raises his revolver and shoots
him. CAPTAIN JACK holds his heart and skips
back to his place among the chiefs.)

CAPTAIN JACK (shaking his fist): Even the stones
you wanted, even the stones!

(The pianist strikes up the chords, the drummers
drum. Old CHIEF JOSEPH walks into the spot
and stands in front of GENERAL CROOK, then
he mimes walking.)

JOSEPH: General One-Armed Howard, why are you
following me?

GENERAL CROOK: The President has ordered that
you move out of Wallowa Valley.

JOSEPH: But two years ago the Great White Father
promised the Nez Percés this land for ever.

GENERAL CROOK: He cannot control the settlers.

They come and they come.

JOSEPH: But he can control the Indians? Are we better children?

GENERAL CROOK: The government has set aside a reservation and you must go in it.

JOSEPH: The land is part of our bodies. We never give up the earth, for it would be like giving up ourselves.

GENERAL CROOK: I don't want to offend your religion but you must talk about practical things. Twenty times over I hear that the earth is your mother and about chieftainship from the earth. I want to hear no more but to come to business at once.

JOSEPH: Who can tell me what I must do in my own country?

(GENERAL CROOK spurs his horse on. JOSEPH starts to run (on the spot).)

GENERAL CROOK: You have thirty days to move!

JOSEPH: Why are you in such a hurry? I cannot get my people ready in that time. The Snake River is very high and our stock is scattered . . .

(JOSEPH slows down to a walk.)

GENERAL CROOK (prodding JOSEPH with his toe): Listen, you red bastard, if you let the time run over by one day the soldiers will be there to drive you on to the reservation and all your cattle and horses left outside will fall into the hands of the white men!

77

(JOSEPH starts to run again.)

JOSEPH: So I led my people into the Bitterroot
    Mountains. We were going to run for Canada.
    The soldiers followed. We ran and we ran and
    we ran. They caught us and killed us, then we
    ran again, we ran through the winter.
    (GENERAL CROOK gallops after JOSEPH,
    waving his sabre.)

GENERAL CROOK: Come back! Come back! The
    Great White Father commands!

JOSEPH: Then came the time when there was no
    more running in us. We were spent.
    (JOSEPH falls to the ground. GENERAL CROOK
    looks down on him from his horse.)

GENERAL CROOK: If you will give up your arms I
    will spare your lives and send you to your
    reservation. I am not a hard man.

JOSEPH: General Howard, I know your heart. What
    you told me before I have in my heart. Our
    chiefs are killed. The old men are all dead. It
    is cold and we have no blankets. The little
    children are freezing to death. I am tired, my
    heart is sick and sad. From where the sun now
    stands I will fight no more for ever.
    (Pause. GENERAL CROOK slumps forward on
    his horse, then straightens up.)

GENERAL CROOK: I am not General Howard, dammit!
    I am none of these men! I am myself and I tried
    to help the Indian. I did what I could. You know

78

damn well how I tried!

(BIG FOOT stumbles forward into the spot, hugging himself, flapping his arms, blowing his fingers.)

BIG FOOT: Oh it was cold, Colonel Forsyth, oh it was cold! You drove us hard remember, sir, God Almighty! Taking us to prison in Omaha. The night before the big killing you drank whisky because you had captured old Big Foot, already I was spitting blood and dead. But you drank on. In the morning you panicked and shot us, Colonel Forsyth.

GENERAL CROOK: I'm not Colonel Forsyth, dammit! I'm Crook!

(BIG FOOT throws himself at the foot of the horse and lies in a grotesque posture, arms and legs raised.)

BIG FOOT: This is how they found me, Colonel Forsyth. You shot us down and we froze like this, and this, and this . . . (He mimes a series of poses.) Why? We were poor, nearly dead with the great cold, I was leading what was left of my people to find peace. Why shoot old Big Foot? Was it our faces? Our smell? The way we sat our ponies when we had them? Were we vermin to be killed like rats in the barn? Where did you find this hatred?

GENERAL CROOK: Get up!

BIG FOOT: I am dead, Three-Stars. I am frozen!

79

My limbs will not move!

GENERAL CROOK: This isn't fair! I tried to help!
I did everything I could within the bounds of my
duty as a soldier. Give me credit when it's due.
Was there another soldier in the United States
Army who tried to help the Indian like I did?
(BIG FOOT crawls away, looking back at CROOK.
Pause. STANDING BEAR steps forward and
puts a hand on CROOK'S arm.)

STANDING BEAR: It is true.

GENERAL CROOK: Thank you, Standing Bear. Tell
them what I did for the Poncas.

STANDING BEAR: In the Moon of the Red Grass
Appearing the Great Father gave us a new reservation on the bank of the Arkansas. We walked
150 miles to this place. Then we were all sick
and many died. Soon I had one son left to die
and he did die. When he was dying he made me
promise to bury him in our old burial ground
by the Swift Running Water. I put his body in a
box and in a waggon and I took my dead son
north. By that time it was the Snow Thaws
Moon. The soldiers caught us and put us in the
fort in chains.

GENERAL CROOK: I went to Fort Omaha to see
them. I was appalled by the conditions under
which the Poncas were being held.

STANDING BEAR: "Gray Wolf," I said to him then,
"I thought God intended us to live, but I was

80

mistaken. God intends to give the country to the white people and we are to die. It may be well: it may be well."

GENERAL CROOK: I went to the Press. I mounted a campaign. I went so far as to arrange a trial - Crook versus Standing Bear - whereby a judge would issue a writ of Habeas Corpus upon me to bring my Ponca prisoners into court and show by what authority I held them.

(The vaulting horse is shoved off to alcove R. A judge's chair is brought on centre upper level. The CHIEFS crowd around the chair on the lower level, giving room for CROOK and STANDING BEAR. Enter JUDGE DUNDY, who takes the chair.)

JUDGE DUNDY: This court is now in session. General George Crook, I have issued a writ of Habeas Corpus on you?

GENERAL CROOK: You have, your honour.

JUDGE DUNDY: Why are you holding Standing Bear of the Poncas as a prisoner?

GENERAL CROOK: He is off his reservation. He is an Indian.

JUDGE DUNDY: Who says he must stay on this "reservation"?

GENERAL CROOK: The government. The government tells him where to live.

JUDGE DUNDY: But this man has no voice in the government?

GENERAL CROOK: He has no rights, your honour. The Fourteenth Amendment gave Negroes equal rights but not Indians. He is also, by law, an alien.

JUDGE DUNDY: How the hell can he be an alien if he was born here?

GENERAL CROOK: He is an Indian.

JUDGE DUNDY: Let's get this straight. You're saying that this man was born here, lives here, yet he's got no rights? That's not what the Declaration of Independence says, is it, General? Remember?

GENERAL CROOK: I do.

JUDGE DUNDY: Well, if you remember, let's have it.

GENERAL CROOK (pause): We hold these truths to be self-evident: that all men are created equal . . .

JUDGE DUNDY: That's enough. So the case rests on one fine point. Is this person a man? Are you a man?

STANDING BEAR: I am a man.

JUDGE DUNDY: Then you have the right to avail yourself of the rights of freedom guaranteed by the Constitution.

GENERAL CROOK: But he is subject to government legislation concerning tribal Indians. They are a special case.

JUDGE DUNDY (standing up): If you don't keep quiet, General, I'll make you a special case. You'll

be the first General that I've fined a hundred
dollars for contempt of court! Release Standing
Bear! He is a free man!

(The CHIEFS jump up and chair STANDING
BEAR around the theatre in a wild demonstration.
JUDGE DUNDY exits. GENERAL CROOK returns
to his alcove. The CHIEFS bring STANDING
BEAR back and resume their positions around
the stage and auditorium. Pause.)

CRAZY HORSE: One month later Great Warrior
Sherman undid that law. He put aside this
Constitution, he put aside these rights, he said
that no Ponca was a man. It was Standing Bear's
brother Big Snake who tried out this law again
and the Army broke it. At Fort Reno they shot
Big Snake dead and showed us the truth again.
The Indian was an alien in his own land.

GENERAL CROOK (sitting on his stool): I tried . . .

CRAZY HORSE: One half of you tried, the man. Then
you were part Indian, but it did not last long.
(The pianist plays the chords with full fortiss-
imo and SITTING BULL steps into the spot. The
drummers drum. SITTING BULL holds up his
hand.)

SITTING BULL: I am Tatanta Yotanka, the Sitting
Bull, chief of the Hunkpapa Sioux and the most
famous Indian of all time. There is no one here
who has not heard of me! My deeds are known
throughout the world. I have one story and it is

not about my victories, my intellect, my powerful medicine, my numerous talents, my illustrious
friends such as Buffalo Bill Cody and the Pope -
my story is none of these. My story is a travel
story. I was such a well-known figure in American
politics that the Great White Father invited me
to go to the East and I went to the great city of
New York in the year of the white man's reck-
oning 1885. There I was taken for a journey on
the waters and I saw a thing that amazed my eye
and puzzled my mind - not an easy thing to do to
Sitting Bull. On an island the whites had built a
figure of a great squaw with a torch held up like
this, and a book in her other hand. It was the
biggest squaw I had ever seen, she touched the
clouds. At her feet were broken chains. We
sailed to the very ground on which the squaw
stood and I was shown some writing on a mighty
block of stone. It was a poem and it was long
and I remember little poetry but my own, but I
remember these words . . .

(The CHIEFS sink to the ground, squat, hug
themselves as if against the cold.)

> Give me your tired, your poor,
> Your huddled masses yearning to
> breathe free.

(Pause. SITTING BULL turns round and looks
at CROOK.)

SITTING BULL: You have seen this?

84

GENERAL CROOK: I have seen it.

SITTING BULL: Who is the squaw speaking to? Her
    face is towards the East, she looks across the
    sea.

GENERAL CROOK (unable to look SITTING BULL in
    the eye): She talks to the whites who are unhappy
    in their own country. It is called the Statue of
    Liberty.

SITTING BULL: Ah, Liberty. Now I see. The squaw
    was therefore not including us. The puzzlement
    has gone. (He goes to walk away but suddenly
    turns on CROOK, his voice harsh and angry.)
    Do not tell me that you tried! We tried! We
    signed papers until our hands ached! We went to
    councils! We listened to commissioners! We
    gave you our land so we could have peace! You
    behaved as though you had given your word to
    children! The Great White Father killed his
    sons and daughters even when they were poor
    and in rags!

GENERAL CROOK: I respected you as men and
    warriors. What other recognition can a soldier
    give?

SITTING BULL: Crazy Horse, tell Three Stars God
    Almighty what his brother officer Sheridan said
    about The People.

CRAZY HORSE: He said that the only good Indian is
    a dead Indian.

SITTING BULL: By this time we were nearly all

good Indians. We were all ready for death, until
we heard the Word, the Ghost Dance.

(WOVOKA takes the centre-stage, dancing. He
acts like a mad prophet, full of passion and
rage but clear and articulate. He runs from
centre round to all the CHIEFS, doing the strange
side-to-side Ghost Dance. CROOK covers his
eyes.)

WOVOKA: Christ is an Indian! Who says Christ is
white? I have sent for you to see me, the
Messiah! I am going to talk to you about all
your fathers and mothers, all your brothers
and sisters who are dead. They are coming
back. My children, I will teach you how to
dance this dance and I want you to dance it.
Get ready for your dance . . .

(All the CHIEFS copy WOVOKA and follow him
in the Ghost Dance. They do a big circle and
resume their positions - now they are with
WOVOKA, eager to hear what he has to say.)

SITTING BULL: Hear him! Hear the Christ!

WOVOKA: In the beginning God made the earth and
he sent Christ to teach the people but white men
treated him badly, leaving scars on his body,
and so he returned to Heaven. Now he has come
back as an Indian. I will renew the earth and
make it better! Dance!

(The CHIEFS dance again, following WOVOKA,
down the aisles, round the back of the auditorium,

and return to the lower level. WOVOKA jumps
on to the upper level.)

WOVOKA: The earth will have fresh soil! The fresh
soil will bury the white men and then be covered
with new grass, running water and trees. The
buffalo will return. All you Indians who dance
the Ghost Dance with me will rise into the air
while this new world is in the making. When
you are set down again all your dead friends
will be with you. The land will belong to the
Great Spirit again and he will give it to The
People.

GENERAL CROOK: This is madness. This man's a
charlatan, a hoaxer! Dammit, you can't put the
clock back! Don't listen to him!
(The CHIEFS form a circle round CROOK and
do the Ghost Dance. The rhythm becomes
insistent, deeper. The eyes of the CHIEFS glaze,
they are dancing in a trance. Only CRAZY
HORSE remains outside the circle.)

WOVOKA: Who are The People?

CHIEFS: We are The People!

WOVOKA: Who is the Christ?

CHIEFS: You are the Christ!

GENERAL CROOK: In God's name, Crazy Horse,
stop this mumbo-jumbo! Do you want another
war on your hands?

CRAZY HORSE: Gray Wolf, if I had been allowed to
live that long, if I had not been cut down with

the bayonet while a prisoner . . .

GENERAL CROOK: That was not my doing!

CRAZY HORSE: You are all the pony-soldiers, Gray
Wolf. You are all your people and we are ours.
If I had lived in the time of the Ghost Dance, I
would have done it! I would have danced! Even
if I knew there was no chance of its being the
Truth I would have been a Ghost Dancer and
followed the prophet Wovoka!

GENERAL CROOK: This situation is getting out of
control.

CRAZY HORSE (leaping into the circle of Ghost
Dancers): Hopo hook-ahay!
(The rhythm mounts and the circle gets closer
to CROOK. CRAZY HORSE leaps and twirls
with a dance of his own but keeping in line.
Suddenly he crouches and points a finger at
CROOK. The dancers stop. Freeze.)

CRAZY HORSE: You had come to our sacred ground,
the centre of The People's world. The Black
Hills were the last home of the Great Spirit and
you came even there looking for gold! If I dug
up the floors of your churches looking for metal,
what would you do?

GENERAL CROOK: You couldn't expect us to take
your religion seriously. It was mere super-
stition. There was no logic to it! Dammit!

CRAZY HORSE: Ha! Three in one and one in three!
Virgin Mary with child!

88

(CRAZY HORSE leaps into the air and the Ghost Dance starts again, creeping closer to the vaulting horse. The CHIEFS are now very close to CROOK, brushing his boots as they dance round him. CRAZY HORSE springs into the air and lands in a crouch, pointing at CROOK again. The dance pauses.)

CRAZY HORSE: Who came after me up the Powder River into the holy Black Hills? Who helped the Great White Father break his word?

CHIEFS: Gray Wolf!

CRAZY HORSE: Who beat General Three Stars God Almighty Crook at the Battle of the Rosebud?

CHIEFS: Crazy Horse!

CRAZY HORSE: We loved the Black Hills, oh we loved that land. It was our heart and our middle. You came and fought us on behalf of thieves. You were paid by thieves! Where are the two men now? A soldier is a soldier and if his honour is sold for gold then that is the kind of soldier he is! If I had the naming of you I would have called you Golden Calf!

(GENERAL CROOK strikes out at CRAZY HORSE in a rage. The CHIEFS crowd round him and pull him off the vaulting horse.

CRAZY HORSE jumps on his back and the CHIEFS force CROOK on to his hands and knees until CRAZY HORSE can get astride him as though on horseback. The CHIEFS then release

(CROOK and stand back. CRAZY HORSE laughs and digs his heels into CROOK'S sides. CROOK behaves like a wild horse - he bucks, leaps, shakes, writhes, trying to dislodge his rider. The neighing of the wild horse fills the theatre. CRAZY HORSE rides out the madness of CROOK until he is still.)

CRAZY HORSE: Now I have you. You are the wild horse of my dream. You are the madness The People have tried to ride. I am on your back and you are quiet. At last I am riding my dream! But too late!

GENERAL CROOK: Let me get up, Crazy Horse!

CRAZY HORSE: No, you are the crazy horse. I am The People and I am going to ride your dreams for ever. You Americans, you Spaniards, you Englishmen, you Frenchmen and Dutchmen, you Portuguese, all of you are saddled with me. I am going to sit across your conscience and be your rider until the world ends.

GENERAL CROOK: This is a child's game! Dammit! Get off my back!

(The CHIEFS spread out on either side of CROOK and CRAZY HORSE. They start making encouraging sounds, as if to a horse, clucking and whistling. CRAZY HORSE whacks CROOK over the backside.)

CRAZY HORSE: Hopo-hook-ahay America! Giddiap! We should have ridden you before!

(Slowly CROOK starts to shuffle forward with CRAZY HORSE on his back. The CHIEFS fall into line behind them. CROOK goes down the aisle on all fours. He moves very slowly and painfully. CRAZY HORSE starts the mourning song.)

CRAZY HORSE: Where are the Tainos now?

CHIEFS: Where are the People?

CRAZY HORSE: Where are the Arawaks?

CHIEFS: Where are the People?

CRAZY HORSE: Where are the Aztecs?

CHIEFS: Where are the People?

CRAZY HORSE: Where are the Incas?

(As the CHIEFS go down the aisle they should try to involve the audience in the mourning song "Where are the People?" At the same time the pianist mounts the upper level, finds the white-wash and brush and paints in the remaining portions of the Americas.)

CHIEFS: Where are the People? (The refrain is repeated after each tribe.)

CRAZY HORSE: Where are the Tainos?

Where are the Arawaks?

Where are the Aztecs?

Where are the Incas?

Where are the Wampanoags?

Where are the Pequots?

Where are the Narragansets?

Where are the Ottawas?

Where are the Shawnees?
Where are the Miamis?
Where are the Foxes?
Where are the Chitimichas?
Where are the Taenzas?
Where are the Natchez?
Where are the Karoks?
Where are the Yazoos?
Where are the Choctaws?
Where are the Chickasaws?
Where are the Bilox?
Where are the Seminoles?
Where are the Apalachees?
Where are the Modocs?
Where are the Apaches?
Where are the Mohaves?
Where are the Paiutes?
Where are the Shastas?
Where are the Yuma?
Where are the Navahoes?
Where are the Utes?
Where are the Osages?
Where are the Pawnees?
Where are the Poncas?
Where are the Santees?
Where are the Cheyennes?
Where are the Teton Sioux?
Where are the Arapahoes?
Where are the Kiowas?

Where are the Comanches?
Where are the Nez Percés?
Where are the Brulés?
Where are the Minneconjous?
Where are the Oglala Sioux?
Where are the People?

(As the last CHIEF exits, the pianist paints in
the last portion of the map. He then exits. By
this time the lights have dimmed down and only
the moon is illuminated. It darkens, goes out.)

39/104